Esquire

The
Rules

A Man's Guide to Life

HEARST BOOKS

A division of Sterling Publishing Co., Inc.

New York / London
www.sterlingpublishing.com

Copyright © 2003, 2005, 2008 by Hearst Communications, Inc.

All rights reserved.

Design: Elizabeth Van Itallie

The Library of Congress has cataloged the original edition as follows:
Esquire:the rules:a man's guide to life/ the editors of Esquire magazine:
Foreword, David Granger.
        p. cm.
Includes index.
        ISBN 1-58816-244-3
Conduct life—Humor 2. American wit and humor
        I. Esquire, inc.
PN6231.C6142 E68 2003
818' .60208—dc21   2002151187

10 9 8 7 6 5 4 3 2 1

Third Edition 2008
Published by Hearst Books, A Division of Sterling Publishing Co., Inc. 387 Park Avenue South, New York, NY 10016

Esquire and Hearst Books are trademarks of Hearst Communications, Inc.

www.esquire.com

For information about custom editions, special sales, premium and corporate purchases,
please contact Sterling Special Sales Department at 800-805-5489 or specialsales@sterlingpub.com.

Distributed in Canada by Sterling Publishing C/o Canadian Manda Group, 165 Dufferin Street,
Toronto, Ontario, Canada M6K 3H6

Distributed in Australia by Capricorn Link (Australia) Pty. Ltd., P.O. Box 704, Windsor, NSW 2756 Australia

Manufactured in China

Sterling ISBN 13: 978-1-58816-693-7
      ISBN 10: 1-58816-693-7

Acknowledgments

Esquire's Rule-makers include:

Ted Allen

Tim Carvell

Matthew Belloni

Matt Claus

Brian Frazer

David Granger

Lauren Iannotti

A.J. Jacobs

David Jacobson

David Katz

Peter Martin

Scott Omelianuk

Evan Rothman

Mike Sachs

David Walters

Andy Ward

Foreword

Seven years ago, up in *Esquire*'s research library, behind the Periodicals Index and stacks of old issues of *Popular Mechanics*, we discovered a leather-bound, hand-calligraphed tome. Engraved in the leather cover were two simple words: **The Rules**.

Since that day, on the third Tuesday of every month, a staff member has made his pilgrimage to the Book. He opens it, jots down whichever maxims catch his eye and scurries back to his cubicle. We then, month after month, offer our findings to our faithful readers.

At first glance, some of them appear to be more opinion (Rule No. 191: The best instrument is the cello). Some appear to be the products of moments of exasperation with the world (Rule No. 659: The dumber the man, the louder he talks). Others the product of moments of enthusiasm or hysteria (Rule No. 206: It's always time for pie). But, no, these are rules.

They have stood the test of time, and they have been bound between the covers of a *book*. They are, therefore, true.

What we at *Esquire*, the magazine, try to do month after month is mix the lessons the world hurls at us on a daily basis with a sense of the absurd. The rules contained herein may not be a guide to every single facet of a man's life, but they provide a way—through either advice or humor—to get through most of it, one rule at a time.

What we offer here is an expanded version of our original rules book. It is just a fraction of the plenitude of wisdom contained in the rules. More will leach out, on the third Tuesday of each month, and find its way into the magazine one month at a time.

Courage,

David Granger
Editor in Chief

Rule No. 1
In an argument between two men, the one chewing a cigar naturally has the upper hand.

Rule No. 2
When someone says he is "pumped" about something, it usually means he's about to do something stupid.

Rule No. 3
The rearview mirror mounted to your computer at work cannot prevent mockery from sneaking up on you.

Rule No. 4
Do not trust a man who calls the bathroom "the little boys' room."

Rule No. 5
When aliens talk, they never use contractions.

Rule No. 6
Women who sound sexy on the radio weigh 377 pounds.

Rule No. 7
If you must use a euphemism for masturbation, the only appropriate one is "scalping General Custer."

Rule No. 8
For every Tom Hanks, there's a Peter Scolari.

Rule No. 9
Wow is not a verb.

Rule No. 10
Sitcom characters watching porn always tilt their heads.

Rule No. 11
People who habitually mark e-mails as "urgent" usually possess neither the authority to send an urgent e-mail nor the intelligence to tell the difference.

Rule No. 12
Goji berry is the funniest berry.

Rule No. 13
In movies Italians can play Jews, and Jews can play Italians, but neither Jews nor Italians can play Lutherans.

Rule No. 14
Actors are short. Comedians are shorter.

Rule No. 15
There is nothing that can be marketed that cannot be better marketed using the voice of James Earl Jones.

Rule No. 16
No talking at the urinal.

Rule No. 17
While on a date, the words snatch, prick, and crack should only be used as verbs.

Rule No. 18
There is an exactly 2-percent chance that you will be seated next to a beautiful, single woman on your next flight.

Rule No. 19
Less if you're flying first class. Then again, who cares— it's first class.

Rule No. 20
No group of people has worse hairstyles than men in government.

Rule No. 21
White cars look good only on *Fantasy Island*.

Rule No. 22
New findings will dictate that eggs are alternately good and bad for you every 4.3 years.

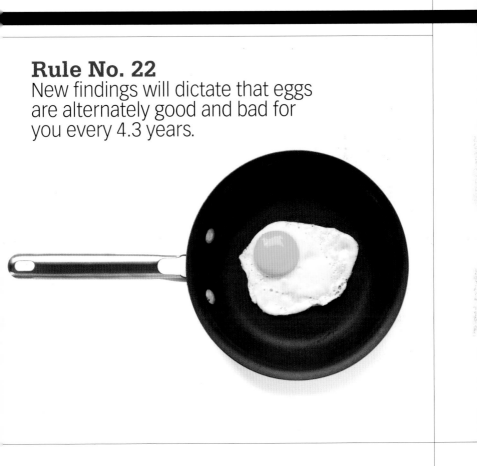

Rule No. 23

If you become annoyed with a telephone customer-service representative, be aware that the words "I'd like to speak to your supervisor" are generally understood to mean "I'd like to speak to your friend in the next cubicle who will pretend to be your supervisor." Just so you know.

Rule No. 24

Unless you're a professional cyclist, or have lost a bet, take off the tight black Lycra biking shorts. And then burn them.

Rule No. 25

If Bill Gates were good-looking or well dressed, people would like him better.

Rule No. 26
A man in a minivan
is half a man.

Rule No. 27
A man on a 1949 Indian motorcycle
traveling at 93 miles an hour is 3.729 men,
until he's cloven in twain by a bridge
abutment, at which point he becomes two
halves of a man.

Rule No. 28
If you have been drinking, arrested, or touring a hostile land full of gun-toting fundamentalists, talk one-fifth as much as you listen.

Rule No. 29
No matter how furtive or quick the glance, a woman always knows when you're looking at her breasts.

Rule No. 30
If you are a mentally retarded character in a movie, it is imperative that your pants be too short.

Rule No. 31
There is no shame in a good mango.

Rule No. 32
Talk half as much as you listen.

Rule No. 33
If a girl breaks up with you because you call her crazy, you were probably right in the first place.

Rule No. 34
The best force is centrifugal.

Rule No. 35
The only good white, dreadlocked street musician playing an extended reggae version of "Tears in Heaven" is a dead white, dreadlocked street musician playing an extended reggae version of "Tears in Heaven."

Rule No. 36
No matter how hard you practice, you cannot say the phrase, "Yeah, right" without sounding sarcastic.

Rule No. 37
There is no shame in the peanut butter sandwich.

Rule No. 38
When it comes to luggage, men don't pull.

Rule No. 39
People will compliment you on the cheap artwork you purchased at IKEA, but it will feel hollow.

Rule No. 40
Never cook with wine bought at a grocery store and labeled "cooking wine."

Rule No. 41
Never cook with wine that you wouldn't want to drink.

Rule No. 42
If you drink only Chateau Latour, never cook.

Rule No. 43
For the last time, no goddamn Speedos.

Rule No. 44
The best vocal register is basso profundo.

Rule No. 45
There comes a time in every man's life when airborne livestock is no longer funny.

Rule No. 46
No man's blender is getting enough use these days.

Rule No. 47
There is no dignified way to ask why you weren't invited to the pool party.

Rule No. 48
There are few arguments between friends that cannot be resolved with a quick Google search.

Rule No. 49
It is unnecessary to compound the effect of white shoes by wearing a white belt.

Rule No. 50
The soft taco is the only taco that matters.

Rule No. 51
When introducing yourself, you will not amuse anyone by adding, "And I'm an alcoholic."

Rule No. 52
The slang used by teens in TV dramas is exactly 3.5 years behind actual slang.

Rule No. 53
Orange things have to be round.

Rule No. 54
Offering to rub oil over the semi-naked body of a total stranger is no more appropriate on the beach than at a bar mitzvah.

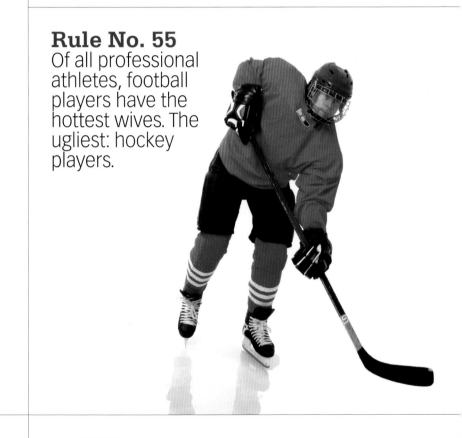

Rule No. 55
Of all professional athletes, football players have the hottest wives. The ugliest: hockey players.

Rule No. 56
No one looks cool
playing the paddle
game.

Rule No. 57
The study of inert
gases is best left to
professionals.

Rule No. 58
Never trust anyone
who, within five
minutes of meeting
you, tells you where
he went to college.

Rule No. 59
Especially if he
refers to his college
as "a little school
in Boston" followed
by a pause as he
waits for you to ask
its name.

Rule No. 60
A sandwich tastes exactly one-third better when it's made by someone else.

Rule No. 61
Drugstores have the slowest cashiers.

Rule No. 62
No mammals on the sweaters. Or belts.

Rule No. 63
People with state pride are to be strictly avoided.

Rule No. 64
The guy in the gorilla suit gets sweaty, not lucky.

Rule No. 65
No squatting in public.

Rule No. 66
Women named after a month of the year are usually frisky.

Rule No. 67
Two-percent milk is bullshit.

Rule No. 68
No matter how greasy the pizza is, you can't blot it with a paper towel and expect to be taken seriously.

Rule No. 69

Unless you are a member of the extended Windsor family, your summer house should not have a name like Emmerdale or Turkey Hill.

Rule No. 70

Come to think of it, the Clapper still isn't cool.

Rule No. 71

Never trust an act of civil disobedience led by a disc jockey.

Rule No. 72
People who tell you
they love the taste
of eggplant are lying.

Rule No. 73
Never trust a man
who uses nautical
metaphors.

Rule No. 74
From least chaotic
to most chaotic:
willy-nilly, hugger-
mugger, hurly-burly,
pell-mell.

Rule No. 75
The ampersand
should be more
popular.

Rule No. 76
The sniffing of one's finger is a pleasure best indulged discreetly.

Rule No. 77
Inviting others to sniff one's finger: more discreetly still.

Rule No. 78
A man whose belt is fastened on the last hole is a desperate and resourceless-looking man.

Rule No. 79
It's possible to actually become dumber by watching TV newsmagazines.

Rule No. 80
The only thing worse than words ending in "ly" are words ending in "ize."

Rule No. 81
Never trust a man
with two first
names.

Rule No. 82
It then follows that
you should steer
well clear of Philip
Michael Thomas.

Rule No. 83
The last slice of
pie is the
tastiest.

Rule No. 84
Never trust a man with pictures of balloons on his cheeks.

Rule No. 85
There is no shame in club soda and cranberry juice.

Rule No. 86
The assassin's compact, high-powered rifle must be packaged in a briefcase by Zero Halliburton.

Rule No. 87
There is nothing more fun than watching young couples in movies visit instant-photo booths.

Rule No. 88
Never trust a man named after a body part.

Rule No. 89
Especially if that body part is a pinkie.

Rule No. 90
More Calvin, less Hobbes.

Rule No. 91
Stewardesses from Third World airlines are much more attractive than those from developed nations.

Rule No. 92
Only the very rich can use summer and winter as verbs.

Rule No. 93
Not even the Sultan of Brunei can use autumn as a verb.

Rule No. 94
Just because Foreigner is playing at a small venue near you tonight, and there are still tickets available, doesn't mean you should go.

Rule No. 95
People who live inland are fatter than those who live in coastal areas.

Rule No. 96
The *Wall Street Journal* is the proper newspaper for the steam room.

Rule No. 97
Never play cards with a man who wears a visor.

Rule No. 98
Shortstops are the best-looking baseball players, followed by first basemen and pitchers, in that order.

Rule No. 99
Right fielders are the ugliest.

Rule No. 100
Lips that have actually been stung by bees are not all that erotic.

Rule No. 101
Never trust a man who claps backs.

Rule No. 102
When it comes to author photos, hands should be at least eight inches from the face.

Rule No. 103
A man over the age of 30 should not pick a fistfight by thrusting out his neck, flexing, and screaming "It's go time!" to passersby.

Rule No. 104
A man may own
exactly one pair of
holiday-themed
boxers.

Rule No. 105
That holiday should
not be Secretary's
Day.

Rule No. 106
Born-again
Christians have the
most meticulously
parted hair.

Rule No. 107
Yams are the most under-appreciated tuber.

Rule No. 108
Beau is the most under-appreciated Bridges.

Rule No. 109
The road to hell is not paved with good intentions. The road to hell is paved with smooth-jazz CDs, herbal teas, John Tesh specials, and low-fat cheese.

Rule No. 110
As a man gets older, his glasses and ears get larger at exactly the same rate.

Rule No. 111
There is no shame in rum-raisin ice cream.

Rule No. 112
No movie should have its title incorporated into the dialogue.

Rule No. 113
The outcome of
no sporting event is
worth punching
a wall.

Rule No. 114
Unless you are a
Pilgrim, large shoe
buckles are to be
avoided.

Rule No. 115
Tollbooths are not for the asking of directions.

Rule No. 116
The best blind dates are with girls named Kelly or Samantha.

Rule No. 117
White basketball players should be extraordinarily white and should have bad hair.

Rule No. 118
"Before" models are more likely to respond to fan mail.

Rule No. 119
Central and Middle America have similar names, but, in reality, they are very different.

Rule No. 120
Words that end in "oma" (e.g., melanoma) are bad.

Rule No. 121
Your car never runs better, faster, or smoother than just after it's washed.

Rule No. 122
Trust no one who uses unusual paper clips.

Rule No. 123
Designer eyeglasses should make you look like something between a German architect and a Libyan dictator.

Rule No. 124
Hip Asians are hipper than people from any other ethnic group.

Rule No. 125
Nobody named "Josh" is over 35.

Rule No. 126
Fried calamari is invariably disappointing.

Rule No. 127
People with alliterative first and last names aren't in on the joke.

Rule No. 128
Unemployed men who dress as if they're unemployed tend to stay unemployed.

Rule No. 129
When it comes to personalized stationery, men don't have it.

Rule No. 130
Never trust a man who uses a vibrato while singing "Happy Birthday."

Rule No. 131
There is nothing funnier than cussing puppets.

Rule No. 132
You must publish three books with the phrase "bathroom reader" in the title in order to feel the pride you would from publishing one without.

Rule No. 133
There is so much
a mustache says
about a man.

Rule No. 134
And none of it
is good.

Rule No. 135
Be wary of people who address their dad as "Father."

Rule No. 136
Be even more wary of people who address their dad as "Colonel."

Rule No. 137
Slow-motion violence goes best with the work of Gustav Mahler.

Rule No. 138
No man can own a longhaired cat and still command respect.

Rule No. 139
Gratuitous nazi-bashing never goes out of style.

Rule No. 140
Wishing we were still united in a supercontinent known as Pangaea is not the best use of your time.

Rule No. 141
Every great poet has, at least once, described the ocean as undulating.

Rule No. 142
A man should avoid using the phrase "assume the position" on the first date.

Rule No. 143
A papasan chair is discarded in the United States every 7.5 seconds.

Rule No. 144
Doric are the best columns.

Rule No. 145
Never allow your fashion sense to be dictated by "island" culture.

Rule No. 146
Anyone who reads the *Hollywood Reporter* in public is a jackass.

Rule No. 147
Chest hair will be back in style by autumn 2010.

Rule No. 148
The study of plate tectonics is best left to professionals.

Rule No. 149
All directors named Todd are critically acclaimed.

Rule No. 150
Never begin an essay with a quote from the Bible.

Rule No. 151
Especially Deuteronomy.

Rule No. 152
You will make friends by jumping on the anti–Andrew Lloyd Webber bandwagon.

Rule No. 153
The best vowel modifier is the umlaut.

Rule No. 154
When in doubt, go bowling.

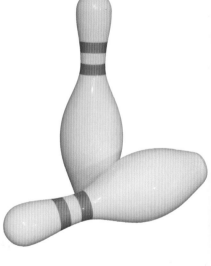

Rule No. 155
Properly made, leftover chili gets better and better every day until the fourth day, at which point it begins its slow decline.

Rule No. 156
Never name a child after a continent,
a nation, or a commonwealth.

Rule No. 157
Or after a body
of water.

Rule No. 158
Especially if that
body of water is
a canal.

Rule No. 159
Never date a woman whose father calls her "princess."

Rule No. 160
Or whose father calls her "butch."

Rule No. 161
There are a million restaurants you want to eat at, which means that when the time comes to pick one, you will be able to think of exactly zero.

Rule No. 162
No straws.

Rule No. 163
The best shape is the rhombus.

Rule No. 164
More nougat.

Rule No. 165
If your physician prefers to be addressed as "Dr. [first name here]," get a second opinion.

Rule No. 166
People who use the word "classy" aren't.

Rule No. 167
The only time it's acceptable for a man to shut one eye is when he's taking a picture.

Rule No. 168
The comma and the colon are the only acceptable punctuation in movie titles.

Rule No. 169
"Partner" is a noun, not a verb.

Rule No. 170
The Nova Scotia duck tolling retriever is the most precisely named dog breed.

Rule No. 171
The future has no buttons.

Rule No. 172
You can't think of the Gutenberg Bible without thinking of Steve.

Rule No. 173
Spanish-speaking people can call New York "Nueva York," but English-speaking people can't call Puerto Rico "Richport."

Rule No. 174
The people who elect to perform karaoke are never the people you wish would perform karaoke.

Rule No. 175
The people who choose to be nudists are never the people you wish to be nudists.

Rule No. 176
No matter how good your numbers are, cholesterol is never something to brag about.

Rule No. 177
Loofahs for everyone!

Rule No. 178
Laundry activity shall be outsourced whenever possible.

Rule No. 179
You can't meet a man named "Colin," as in Powell, without thinking, "Well, he could have been named 'Bunghole.'"

Rule No. 180
Never confer on the creepy habits of the tech-support guy via e-mail.

Rule No. 181
You cut the fat, you cut the flavor.

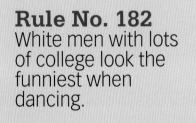

Rule No. 182
White men with lots of college look the funniest when dancing.

Rule No. 183
Women dig preachers.

Rule No. 184

No one finds out you're a tea drinker until after you've got the job.

Rule No. 185

Mayonnaise and Dijon mustard are to be combined on a case-by-case basis.

Rule No. 186

The only thing stupider than the names of hair salons are the names people give their boats. (May we draw your attention to the inordinate number of speedboats called "Wet Dream?")

Rule No. 187
Cairo is the nicest city with open sewers.

Rule No. 188
You don't know anyone named Natasha.

Rule No. 189
Television actors who are also musicians get plotlines that allow them to demonstrate this musical talent on their shows.

Rule No. 190
No one will ever tell you that the chicken salad was not made today.

Rule No. 191
The best instrument is the cello.

Rule No. 192
The most underrated cake is carrot cake.

Rule No. 193
Leaders of religions
get larger houses
and better cars
than followers of
religions.

Rule No. 194
Girl Scout cookies
are for buying,
not eating.

Rule No. 195
Although a failed business is correctly
described as "defunct," it does not follow that
a prosperous business is "funct."

Rule No. 196
No woman over the age of 17 has ever been thrilled by the gift of carnations.

Rule No. 197
Always keep your receipt from RadioShack.

Rule No. 198
The roles Teri Garr used to get now go to Lisa Kudrow.

Rule No. 199
You're not supposed to like your job.

Rule No. 200
Regardless of the vibe you think you're getting from your dentist, you should never lick her finger.

Rule No. 201
No one ever got laid by wearing a sperm costume on Halloween.

Rule No. 202
If your goal is to see a beautiful woman on television, look no further than the Spanish-language networks.

Rule No. 203
Men named Walter are taken more seriously than men named Jason.
Also Billy.

Rule No. 204
Female pastry chefs are to men as male architects are to women.

Rule No. 205
Making a living as a man who turns into a huge green monster with tight, tattered pants to fight crime is fine and dandy—it's your choice. But know this: it's a lonely, lonely life.

Rule No. 206
It's always time for pie!

Rule No. 207
Cranberry sauce is a perfectly good condiment the other 364 days of the year, too.

Rule No. 208
Religion causes
some people to get
really angry and
others to grow long,
funny beards.

Rule No. 209
The long snapper is
the best-named
position in football.

Rule No. 210
Executives don't
need presents.

Rule No. 211
Don't fuck with broccoli.

Rule No. 212
Waiters who sit at your table when they take your order usually get it wrong.

Rule No. 213
You don't have to be a football hero to get along with beautiful girls. Arab princes do okay. Also, short guys with a lot of money.

Rule No. 214
There is nothing that can be marketed that cannot be better marketed using the likeness of Honest Abe Lincoln.

Rule No. 215
People named Gil never win awards.

Rule No. 216
Something changes
in a man when he
brings a cowbell to a
sporting event.

Rule No. 217
It's not a positive
change.

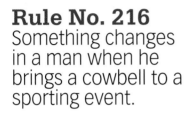

Rule No. 218
Irony doesn't work
on a tombstone.

Rule No. 219
The best looking musician is always the lead singer, followed in descending order by the lead guitarist, rhythm guitarist, drummer, and bass player.

Rule No. 220
There are words to say when playing touch football. "Got you" is fine. "Touchdown," expected. But "Hey, too hard!"—that's a no-no.

Rule No. 221
When intellectuals
are white, they're
called "intellectuals."
When they're black,
they're called "black
intellectuals."

Rule No. 222
The only thing better than a huge, rich company is when a huger, richer company buys it and afterward the CEOs shake hands. They seem so happy that it's kind of contagious.

Rule No. 223
The man who wears a bunny suit is a greater man than the one who wears a business suit.

Rule No. 224
If there's one thing that comes out of a terrible tragedy, it's really dumb legislation.

Rule No. 225
It's interesting to hear about directors' battles with studio executives. Darned studio executives!

Rule No. 226
The best religions have great hats.

Rule No. 227
Crazy men are to be played by Dennis Hopper. Weird men are to be played by Steve Buscemi.

Rule No. 228
A man over the age of 30 should never read a book with the words "Zen and the Art of" in the title.

Rule No. 229
The little extra you pay for name-brand tin foil is well worth it.

Rule No. 230
The last people who should be having kids are always the first to do so.

Rule No. 231
Those who enjoy musical theater should ask themselves, for their own sake and that of their countrymen, "Why?"

Rule No. 232
Melon should be more popular.

Rule No. 233
Yes, seat belts do indeed wrinkle your suit, but so do windshields.

Rule No. 234
When you have a headache and you are tired and you have not slept for 46 hours and will not sleep for 8 more, people will talk louder and in Arabic.

Rule No. 235
Desperate
housewives don't
look like that.

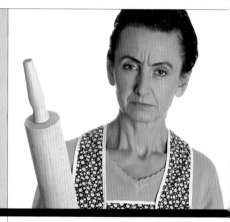

Rule No. 236
A motorcyclist, even
an Irish motorcyclist,
does not want to
hear, "May the road
always rise to meet
you."

Rule No. 237
A PBS tote bag does
not make you an
intellectual.

Rule No. 238
You are not on the team that plays in your city. They are not "we"; their wins are not yours.

Rule No. 239
There is no shame in grape soda.

Rule No. 240
Some women, particularly models, call one another "girls," but you can't.

Rule No. 241
The calla lily is the best flower.

Rule No. 242
The savvy, punctual carpool driver does not offer a travel mug of coffee to the guy who always has to pee.

Rule No. 243
People eager to get married can be trusted about as much as people eager to get elected.

Rule No. 244
For a multitude of reasons, tanned people are not to be trusted.

Rule No. 245
It's okay to be friendly to cops.

Rule No. 246
Flying superheroes get laid the most. Superheroes who swim, the least.

Rule No. 247
People who fish
are very different
from people who
don't fish.

Rule No. 248
After your fifth
divorce, you gotta
start wondering if
maybe it's you.

Rule No. 249
There is nothing
good about berets.

Rule No. 250
There is no shame in well-done steak.

Rule No. 251
It's okay to lie
to liars.

Rule No. 252
To make it really big
on the radio you
need a nickname
along the lines of
Cletus the Fetus.

Rule No. 253
The sexiest fruit is the fig, followed by the peach, the plum, and the pomegranate.

Rule No. 254
The least sexy fruit? The Frankenberry.

Rule No. 255
The bigger the man the smaller the boat.

Rule No. 256
It's not what you
wear or how you
wear it or when
you bought it
or who else has
it. It's what it cost.

Rule No. 257
It's not who you know but how you know
them—and how many other people know who
you know and how you know them. Also
helpful: pictures to prove it.

Rule No. 258
In the parlance of real estate professionals, plants are called "plant materials."

Rule No. 259
In the parlance of airline-industry professionals, cigarettes are called "smoking materials."

Rule No. 260
In the parlance of fashion-industry professionals, a pair of pants is called "a pant."

Rule No. 261
The fatter the man, the smaller the swimsuit.

Rule No. 262
Satan loves parents who give young children rat-tail haircuts.

Rule No. 263
Satan loves parents who dress young children in leather jackets and shades.

Rule No. 264
If you are over 6'3" or under 5'3", you will be asked, "How tall are you?" approximately 4,271 times before you die.

Rule No. 265
Never go home with a woman who smokes cigarillos.

Rule No. 266
The house blend is always hotter than the flavored coffee.

Rule No. 267
People who call ping-pong "table tennis" will always beat you.

Rule No. 268
The longer the limo, the younger the groupies.

Rule No. 269

Any word employed as a prefix for the word "pants" results in a word that is funny, e.g., finickypants, funkypants, happypants, googlypants, nancypants, and boogly-booglypants.

Rule No. 270
Except for
disestablishment-
arianism-pants.
Not funny.

Rule No. 271
Watching the
Academy Awards is
acceptable for a
man. Watching an
arrivals or post-
awards show,
less so.

Rule No. 272
The best number is
7, followed closely
by 9.

Rule No. 273
There is no worst
number; all others
are of equal merit.

Rule No. 274
Pliant people are, more often than not, smarter than stubborn people.

Rule No. 275
But stubborn people are always more effective.

Rule No. 276
Any restaurant that claims on its sign that it's famous probably isn't.

Rule No. 277
The team mascot sleeps alone.

Rule No. 278
If a Halloween costume is unavoidable, it must preserve your good looks, involve no makeup, and be quickly removed in the event of passion.

Rule No. 279
Because even smiling clowns are scary.

Rule No. 280
It's okay if you're
overweight.

Rule No. 281
As long as you can
dance.

Rule No. 282
It is always
unacceptable to
refuse a woman's
request to dance.

Rule No. 283
Especially when she is your mother's age.

Rule No. 284
More especially when she is your mother.

Rule No. 285
The absolute maximum number of times that you can quote Monty Python on a first date and still have a reasonable expectation of getting laid is: zero.

Rule No. 286
If a man is wearing a class ring, do not respect him.

Rule No. 287
If a man is wearing a pinky ring, do not fuck with him.

Rule No. 288
If a man is wearing a ring with the papal insignia on it, then he is the Pope, and try not to curse in front of him.

Rule No. 289
When someone sneezes four times in rapid-fire succession, one "Bless You" will suffice.

Rule No. 290
Before you make fun of the crest on a man's jacket, make sure it's not for his dojo.

Rule No. 291
On any road trip, he who is driving gets control of the radio. No exceptions.

Rule No. 292
Well, if he who is driving is a really big fan of Celine Dion, there should at least be some sort of negotiation.

Rule No. 293
Before getting any sort of tattoo, devote a few minutes' thought to how it will look on your saggy, wrinkled flesh in the nursing home.

Rule No. 294
Never hire a lawyer whose phone number spells the word divorce, injury, or innocent—or their Spanish translations.

Rule No. 295
There is no reason a couple should share one e-mail account.

Rule No. 296
Even the very best "gentlemen's clubs" feel a little bit like sad, sad zoos.

Rule No. 297
Even the very best zoos feel a little bit like animal prisons.

Rule No. 298
Certainly, it is your prerogative to be difficult in restaurants. Just as it's a restaurant worker's prerogative to place unwanted fluids in your meal.

Rule No. 299
If you are uncertain how much cologne is enough, you are not allowed to use cologne.

Rule No. 300
A great cobbler is the closest thing the modern world has to a good wizard.

Rule No. 301
No ponytail, unless you are Willie Nelson.

Rule No. 302

The correct description for any photograph of someone else's baby is "adorable." Have this word ready to go before the photograph is shown, so that, even if the baby is shockingly ugly, you can utter "adorable" without hesitation.

Rule No. 303
The quickest way to impress twins is to be able to figure out which is which.

Rule No. 304
The quickest way to impress triplets is to not spend ten minutes discussing the fact that they're triplets.

Rule No. 305
Umpires will never call or resume a game that has been delayed by rain until you have driven exactly 3.2 miles from the stadium.

Rule No. 306
There is no shame in
milk and cookies.

Rule No. 307
A complicated
coffee order
impresses no one.

Rule No. 308
If you can hear music through the
headphones of the person sitting next
to you, it will never be a song you like.

Rule No. 309
The words "dirt cheap" and "sushi" do not belong in the same sentence—or, rather, if they are in the same sentence, that sentence also often includes "intestinal parasite."

Rule No. 310
Never wave at a video camera.

Rule No. 311
The words "Bruckheimer" and "first date" do not belong in the same sentence.

Rule No. 312
If you're making a sign to be held up at a sporting event, it doesn't hurt to use a dictionary.

Rule No. 313
"Irregardless" is not a word, irregardless of what you say.

Rule No. 314
Be wary the man who shakes your hand while remaining in his seat.

Rule No. 315
There is no shame in eggs for dinner.

Rule No. 316
There is no shame in cinnamon toast.

Rule No. 317
There is, however, ample shame in eating a Lean Cuisine entrée at home, alone, pantless, while watching television. Look at yourself, man. Just look at yourself.

Rule No. 318
Harvard Extension is NOT Harvard.

Rule No. 319
Never select a tattoo simply because it's on sale.

Rule No. 320
If you're younger than 80, you should never utter the phrase "the whole kit and kaboodle."

Rule No. 321
A muffin is just cake in the shape of a mushroom.

Rule No. 322
A power bar is just a candy bar in a shiny wrapper.

Rule No. 323
There's no need to thank someone for their "thank you" card.

Rule No. 324
It's tough to find a
great harmonica
teacher.

Rule No. 325
Food tastes immeasurably better on the
barbecue if you light the fire with those
"Don't Sweat the Small Stuff" books.

Rule No. 326
Jewish comics are really funny in their 20s, 30s, and 40s, not so funny in their 50s and 60s, and then hilarious in their 70s.

Rule No. 327
The weirder the cell phone ring, the more annoying the person.

Rule No. 328
Your child is only 38-percent as cute as you think he is.

Rule No. 329
Here is how movies work: they are filmed on soundstages in California or other fancy locations, and then they are edited, and then, months later, they are sent to your local multiplex.

Rule No. 330
All of which tends to suggest that, when you yell at the heroine on screen, she cannot hear you, no matter how loud you yell, or how important your instructions are to her personal safety.

Rule No. 331
Similarly, if you find yourself really enjoying a movie, and want to applaud when it is over, ask yourself: "What the fuck am I doing?"

Rule No. 332
If you still cook on a hot plate at home it's not gonna be easy to get a car loan.

Rule No. 333
There's no reason to ever say "whoops" out loud.

Rule No. 334
Being a coal miner is tougher than being a coal miner's daughter.

Rule No. 335
Don't wear anything with #1 on it, unless you happen to be Tony Fernandez or Lance Johnson.

Rule No. 336
Quentin is to Tarantino as one-hit is to wonder.

Rule No. 337
Orange marmalade does not qualify as jam.

Rule No. 338
Among the emotions it is impossible to maintain plausibly while wearing leopard-skin clothing: stoicism, ferocity, dourness, studiousness.

Rule No. 339
Wear no leopard-skin clothing. No, not even there.

Rule No. 340
You know you've made it when there's a bobble-head doll of you.

Rule No. 341
Women who tie sweaters around their waists have big asses.

Rule No. 342
Nobody on a political talk show has ever convinced a fellow panelist of anything. Never happened, never will.

Rule No. 343
Having a ferret as a pet doesn't make you any cooler. In fact, it actually makes the ferret less cool.

Rule No. 344
People who used to follow the Grateful Dead across the country are really bored now.

Rule No. 345
They were bored then, too.

Rule No. 346
High-fiving another man at a restaurant could very well be the reason you're single.

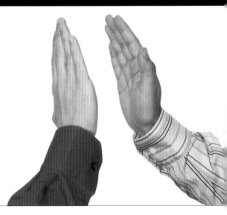

Rule No. 347
Captain Crunch should be Admiral Crunch by now.

Rule No. 348
"We Will Rock You" is the dumbest sports anthem song ever.

Rule No. 349
Walking into Staples and shouting, "Hey, where are the staples?" isn't funny.

Rule No. 350
Pennies are inappropriate at strip clubs.

Rule No. 351
If your head's at the proper angle, smoking actually does make you look cool.

Rule No. 352
Teenagers with
aggressively
asymmetrical hair
get beat up a lot.

Rule No. 353
Do not give yourself
a nickname.

Rule No. 354
Do not make up
your own
catchphrase.

Rule No. 355
No fluorescent
condoms, unless
they're all that's
available.

Rule No. 356
If something has raisins in it, they have to be mentioned in its name.

Rule No. 357
Some chicken doesn't even taste like chicken.

Rule No. 358
Any superhero worth his salt could fly without his cape.

Rule No. 359
You should never be subjected to looking at a man's toes.

Rule No. 360
Dogs with bandanas tied around their necks are not pleased with the accessory.

Rule No. 361
No one should be arrested for keying a car with a vanity plate.

Rule No. 362
Everything is better in a wok.

Rule No. 363
All swimsuit models must complain about shoot conditions in the "making of" documentaries.

Rule No. 364
Americans who say "cheers" are pretentious twits.

Rule No. 365
First class is to business class is to coach as Groucho is to Harpo is to Zeppo.

Rule No. 366
No one likes audiophiles—even other audiophiles.

Rule No. 367
Trendy names are only appropriate if you know your kid is going to be cute.

Rule No. 368
Fat wallet bad; fat money clip good.

Rule No. 369
The mile-high club is silly and sophomoric, but you can say so only if you are a member.

Rule No. 370
A woman's chin and knees are the most underrated parts of her body.

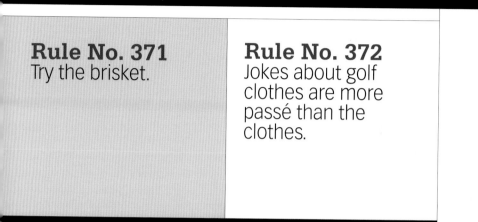

Rule No. 371
Try the brisket.

Rule No. 372
Jokes about golf
clothes are more
passé than the
clothes.

Rule No. 373
Except on the golf
course, golf
umbrellas are
unmanly.

Rule No. 374
Women who have
two or more
brothers are less
likely to be
disgusted by you.

Rule No. 375
You will actually be rewarded in the afterlife for re-gifting.

Rule No. 376
Law firm quality, in descending order: two names, four names, three names, one name, five names.

Rule No. 377
If Steve Buscemi got his teeth fixed he'd probably never work again.

Rule No. 378
Do not argue with the caricaturist.

Rule No. 379
Ninety-seven percent of hockey nicknames are created by adding an "ee" sound to a player's last name.

Rule No. 380
Midget humor is overrated, monkey humor is underrated.

Rule No. 381
Hat-brim bending decreases with age.

Rule No. 382
Character actors have big ears.

Rule No. 383
The French horn at the very beginning of "You Can't Always Get What You Want" is rock's best use of that instrument.

Rule No. 384
Women who come from big families are more fun.

Rule No. 385
That new Bob Dylan album isn't quite as good as everyone says it is.

Rule No. 386
That new Woody Allen film is worse than everyone says it is.

Rule No. 387
It's okay for a man to show up in bed wearing boxers without an undershirt, but never an undershirt without boxers. For a woman, either way is fine.

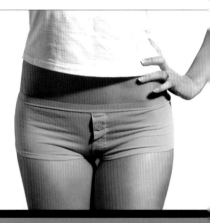

Rule No. 388
Soda tastes 27 percent better from glass bottles than plastic; wine, 79 percent.

Rule No. 389
Nobody comes to watch the coach, no matter what he may think.

Rule No. 390
Avoid restaurants that serve both Chinese and Japanese food.

Rule No. 391
She looks cute tucking her hair behind her ears; you look ridiculous.

Rule No. 392
When in doubt, pick "C."

Rule No. 393

The only thing more important than saying "No, you don't look fat in that outfit" when she asks you the first time, is the deep sincerity with which you must say "Really" when she asks the second time.

Rule No. 394

Sinatra is never wrong.

Rule No. 395

Do not quote Bryan Adams's songs, even ironically.

Rule No. 396
No cameras at the bachelor party, and definitely no video cameras.

Rule No. 397
If it bends, it's funny. If it bends two ways, it's even funnier. If it bends three ways, marry it.

Rule No. 398
The History Channel
is not a substitute
for reading a book
every now and then.

Rule No. 399
Sophisticated
though it may be,
you can't say
"sipping whiskey"
without feeling
goofy.

Rule No. 400
Being hung in effigy
is not a backhanded
compliment.

Rule No. 401
Sharing your ChapStick with a beautiful woman is not the same as making out with her. But it's pretty damn close.

Rule No. 402
History is told by the winners, oral histories are told by old men eating tuna-fish sandwiches in the park.

Rule No. 403
Calling the phone numbers cited in movies or plays will not give you entrée into their fictional worlds.

Rule No. 404
There's no historical basis for Count Chocula.

Rule No. 405
O Brother Where Art Thou? was great. But playing scratchy WPA tapes of guys with three teeth and a junkyard washboard while driving your Lexus RX doesn't actually make you authentically rootsy.

Rule No. 406
There's a special circle in Hell reserved for those who adjust their rearview mirrors while you wait for their parking space.

Rule No. 407
Fishnet stockings made from actual fishnets aren't all that sexy.

Rule No. 408
If you wonder, even momentarily, about the toilet and shower facilities at Burning Man, you're too old to attend.

Rule No. 409
Never mind what time it is, never pose for a "zany" snapshot squatting over Old Faithful.

Rule No. 410
Bald umpires are excellent, no matter the sport.

Rule No. 411
A man wearing a brightly colored fanny pack is seven-eighths of a man.

Rule No. 412
Compulsively clicking "refresh" will not make people e-mail you.

Rule No. 413
A gentleman never considers sexual activity until the dog has been sent to another room.

Rule No. 414
Especially if it's a Jack Russell terrier or could be related to Marmaduke.

Rule No. 415

A man wearing a paper trainee hat is, during the time he has it on, precisely one-sixth of a man.

Rule No. 416

Never attempt "this really cool thing I saw on Animal Planet/Crocodile Hunter/The X Games."

Rule No. 417

A first-date restaurant should never feature an all-you-can-eat salad bar.

Rule No. 418

Never trust a man with more than one umlaut in his name.

Rule No. 419
By now, in all fairness, it should be called Lou Gehrig's and Stephen Hawking's disease.

Rule No. 420
Explaining how your shoes came to be called "wingtips" will not get you laid.

Rule No. 421
Reaching over to flush another man's urinal is universally frowned upon.

Rule No. 422
You will never meet a woman named Rapunzel.

Rule No. 423
If you do, she'll have the shortest, butchiest haircut imaginable.

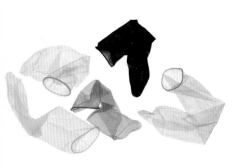

Rule No. 424
Condoms that are red or green or any color but clear will make your manly bits appear to be red or green.

Rule No. 425
Asking her if you can come up "just to use your bathroom," is the Hail Mary pass of romantic moves.

Rule No. 426
Agreeing to "take things slow" is the deep-drop screen pass of romantic moves.

Rule No. 427
Agreeing to date other people "for now," is the punt-on-third-down of romantic moves.

Rule No. 428
From one dude to another: enough with the "dude" already.

Rule No. 429
Every man should know how to make at least one drink from a foreign country, preferably one taught to him by a local female with whom he has had a complicated, unresolved, and quite possibly dangerous alliance.

Rule No. 430
At the checkout counter on your third date, if she says, "Oh wait, we're gonna need chocolate syrup," don't ask what for, just go get it.

Rule No. 431
It's never okay to build or obsessively visit a web site shrine to someone featured in an Apple advertisement.

Rule No. 432
If you're consuming something to flavor your semen, your life has devolved into nothing but a series of tawdry minor amusements.

Rule No. 433
Pretending to get all confused in the elevator and pressing her nipple instead of a floor button will not get you laid.

Rule No. 434
Never discuss affairs of the heart with a guy who refers to sexual intimacy as "my daily requirement of vitamin F."

Rule No. 435
Your Etch-a-Sketch portraits of notable politicians won't get you laid.

Rule No. 436
You are absolutely the only person calling during that PBS pledge break. Every other penny comes from the John D. and Catherine T. MacArthur Foundation and the Chubb Group of Insurance Companies.

Rule No. 437
If you live long enough you will resemble a gargoyle.

Rule No. 438
It's not okay to be in a tribute band to another tribute band.

Rule No. 439
Taxidermists rarely have really hot wives.

Rule No. 440
Explaining why Tesla was actually more brilliant than Edison won't get you laid.

Rule No. 441
Full frontal nudity isn't necessarily sexier than nudity seen from the side.

Rule No. 442
Nobody should name their kids after Melville characters: Not Ishmael. Not Ahab. Not Bartleby. Not Queequeg. Not Tashtego.

Rule No. 443
The day that the *New York Times* referred to Snoop Doggy Dogg on second reference as Mr. Dogg was the day the whole formal news outlet edifice began to crumble.

Rule No. 444
The hottest funk-and-soul metaphors for beautiful women are, in descending order: Brick-houuuse! Little red corvette. Once-twice-three-times a lady.

Rule No. 445
At the holiday office party, consume one drink fewer than your boss.

Rule No. 446
Pretending to conduct an orchestra playing the *Mission Impossible* theme song will not get you laid.

Rule No. 447
There is rarely any genuine need to shout "Skäl!" "Na zdorovye!" "Sláinte!" "Bottoms up!" or "Down the hatch!"

Rule No. 448
A relaxed dress code at work does not legitimize the display of leg hair or chest hair.

Rule No. 449
Any recipe requiring cumin is nothing but hoop-jumping bullshit.

Rule No. 450
Self-expression is not achieved via cartoon-character ties or watches, unless the expression one wishes to achieve is: "loser."

Rule No. 451
To foster its use in your home, call it erotica, not porn.

Rule No. 452
Never utter the words I and love and you if you've had more than three drinks.

Rule No. 453
Only acceptable pick-up line: "Hi, my name is [insert your name], What's yours?"

Rule No. 454
Shorts in the office: only if your office is a wooden chair mounted atop a ladder on a sunny beach and a whistle hangs from around your neck.

Rule No. 455
Love does not mean never having to say you're sorry. It means having to say you're sorry over and over again, in new and different ways, every day, every week, every month, every year, until God grants you his mercy and you finally, blissfully die.

Rule No. 456
No short man was ever named Orlando.

Rule No. 457
Women like a man who likes women who like to eat.

Rule No. 458
Minor league ballparks serve the best hot dogs.

Rule No. 459
The best mogul name ever is T. Boone Pickens.

Rule No. 460
If you're single, the tango will do the trick. If you're married, the tango will also do the trick. Possibly even with your wife.

Rule No. 461
The lower you wear your bass guitar, the cooler you are.

Rule No. 462
Know that while Rhett Butler can get away with telling Scarlett O'Hara that she "should be kissed, and often, and by someone who knows how," you cannot.

Rule No. 463
It is important to avoid rhyming sexual innuendoes such as "urge to merge."

Rule No. 464
And especially "inclination toward copulation."

Rule No. 465
While out on a "buddies only" getaway, 93 percent of all statements can be turned into a "That's what she said" joke.

Rule No. 466
"That's what she said" jokes from men over 40 are only moderately less sad than air guitar.

Rule No. 467
People who begin sentences by saying, "With all due respect," are in fact preparing to impart loads of disrespect.

Rule No. 468
If you own a wild animal, there's a two-in-three chance that you live within walking distance of all your relatives.

Rule No. 469
A man over the age of 30 should not make innuendoes about things that happen to involve the number 69.

Rule No. 470
When a girlfriend and a mouse are in the same room, a man does not belong on the chair.

Rule No. 471
Never trust a man who owns a video of his middle school musical.

Rule No. 472
Never trust a man who knows all the dance steps to "Bye, Bye, Bye."

Rule No. 473
Any actor who uses the word "craft" to refer to acting should be the subject of a public flogging.

Rule No. 474
Go ahead. Be a
vegan. All we ask
is that you do so
quietly.

Rule No. 475
You should never
spend more than
$20 on a pen.

Rule No. 476
Asking "Who had the steak and who had the
fish?" is not the manly way to go about
paying for dinner.

Rule No. 477
There's no thrill like the thrill of getting cash in the mail.

Rule No. 478
Nobody cares about your dreams.

Rule No. 479
A bath in the movies requires at minimum eight candles near the bathtub.

Rule No. 480
The worst color for a new car is red.

Rule No. 481
Conversely, the best color for a new ski boat is red.

Rule No. 482
Practicing half-court shots becomes unacceptable after the age of 14.

Rule No. 483
If there is danger involved, it is fun.

Rule No. 484
It is more fun if it requires you to sign a waiver.

Rule No. 485
The response "you are" is no longer acceptable as a response for the question "what's happening?"

Rule No. 486
No man over the age of 30 should use the word "Dawg" except to refer to a creature with four legs and a leash around its neck.

Rule No. 487
A tattoo of a teardrop is not a sign of sensitivity.

Rule No. 488
Being a regular at Starbucks is nothing to brag about.

Rule No. 489

If your dream involves an elaborate plot in which you are looking for a bathroom, it's time to get up and pee.

Rule No. 490

It's borderline acceptable to spell A.M. as ayem. It's absolutely unacceptable to spell P.M. as peeyem.

Rule No. 491

Scoreboard "races" demean us all.

Rule No. 492

But always bet on green.

Rule No. 493
The best way to get out of a bad date is to claim that you own a ferret.

Rule No. 494
Unless, of course, your date excitedly says that she, too, owns a ferret.

Rule No. 495
Every dish can be improved with the addition of bacon.

Rule No. 496
The appeal of the small, non-corporate, independently owned and operated coffeehouse usually lasts right up until the moment you taste the coffee.

Rule No. 497

If you are a movie character in a hurry and are driving through a rural area, you will run into a herd of sheep crossing the road.

Rule No. 498

A man can never own too many pairs of socks.

Rule No. 499

The slower the movie, the better the reviews.

Rule No. 500
Women whose names end with the letter "i" are more promiscuous.

Rule No. 501
There is nothing worse than a white guy who wants to be a Native American.

Rule No. 502
Mexican restaurants have the worst red wine.

Rule No. 503
Three out of every four short-order cooks have served jail time.

Rule No. 504
When in doubt, give something in a pale blue box.

Rule No. 505
The best dog name is "Rex."

Rule No. 506
The worst cat name is anything beginning with "Mister."

Rule No. 507
People who live in glass houses watch 65 percent less porn.

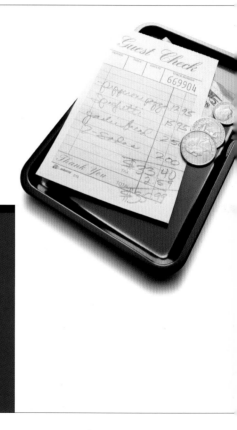

Rule No. 508
After dinner, when you reach into your wallet a little more slowly than everyone else, trust us, they all notice.

Rule No. 509
A self-respecting man should not know how to say anything in Klingon.

Rule No. 510
A self-respecting man should not know how to say anything in Elvish.

Rule No. 511
A self-respecting man should definitely not know the date on which the Olsen twins became legal.

Rule No. 512
The best cinematographers are from Eastern Europe.

Rule No. 513
The best gaffers are from the good old U.S. of A.

Rule No. 514
If you are a contestant on a dating reality show, you must keep at least one minority around until the second round to prove that you aren't racist.

Rule No. 515
If you are a homeless man in the movies, you must wear gloves with the tips of the fingers cut off.

Rule No. 516
Fur hats are appropriate only above the 63rd parallel, unless worn by Sherpas or communists.

Rule No. 517
Three bowling trophies equals one Oscar.

Rule No. 518
Something probably happened in Delaware, but nobody knows what that is, not even people in Delaware.

Rule No. 519
There is no shame in
a really good banana
pudding.

Rule No. 520
There is only mild
shame in a
macchiato.

Rule No. 521
Movies that feature a fat person in the starring role are invariably sad.

Rule No. 522
Or, very, very funny.

Rule No. 523
Just because the bottle says Bath and Body Works for Men doesn't make it right.

Rule No. 524
If you can't make it good, make it big. And if you can't make it big, make it red.

Rule No. 525
The fat kid who brings the Jeter glove to the ballpark to catch a foul—now that's America.

Rule No. 526
Never be the one to start—or finish—a stadium "wave."

Rule No. 527
The lower a waiter bends down when introducing himself, the less he should be trusted.

Rule No. 528
If your PIN number is your girlfriend's birthday, you're a sucker.

Rule No. 529
If your PIN number is your birthday, you're an idiot.

Rule No. 530
Contrary to popular opinion, the word "can't" should be in your vocabulary.

Rule No. 531
The third doughnut is always exactly one and a half doughnuts too many.

Rule No. 532
Avoid any restaurant where the daily specials are displayed by way of plastic replicas.

Rule No. 533
The better looking the person, the more he or she is concerned about the preparation of his or her coffee.

Rule No. 534
Youth-ministry leaders always have goatees.

Rule No. 535
Humor works only on incoming answering-machine messages.

Rule No. 536
Of all military professions, fighter pilots have the best nicknames. The worst: army cooks.

Rule No. 537
The more talented the drummer, the less reliance on dramatic drumstick twirling.

Rule No. 538
The more talented the lead guitarist, the less reliance on the wa-wa pedal.

Rule No. 539
The more talented the singer, the less reliance on colorful microphone scarves.

Rule No. 540
The more talented the lover, the less reliance on colorful condoms.

Rule No. 541
The angrier the man, the more misspellings in his e-mails.

Rule No. 542
Nicknaming your penis with a surname preceded by "Señor" will not make you appear more worldly.

Rule No. 543
If the bartender has a mullet, ordering a martini is probably a bad idea.

Rule No. 544
One exclamation point per e-mail!

Rule No. 545
A man over the age of 30 should not own a futon or a beanbag chair.

Rule No. 546
Avoid any doctor whose middle name appears in quotes.

Rule No. 547
Unless you're a nineteenth-century president, lose the muttonchops.

Rule No. 548
The more important a character in the Bible, the greater his or her capacity for ferocious outbursts of violence against underlings.

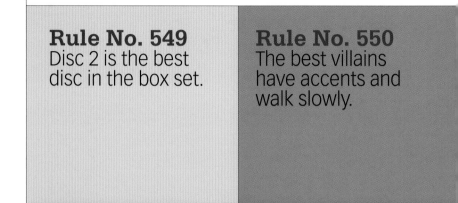

Rule No. 549
Disc 2 is the best
disc in the box set.

Rule No. 550
The best villains
have accents and
walk slowly.

Rule No. 551
When wooing a
woman with your
musical prowess,
never opt for an
accordion, the knee
cymbals, or a lute.

Rule No. 552
The wackier a doctor's neckties, the less prestigious his medical school.

Rule No. 553
Flame decals do not fool passersby into thinking your car is "hot."

Rule No. 554
You don't pay cash at the dentist.

Rule No. 555
If you're in a strip club, and a girl says she's gonna call the manager over, your night just got less fun.

Rule No. 556
People who whine about smoking are just slightly less annoying than people who whine about a ban on smoking.

Rule No. 557
No one's ever gotten laid by wearing pins with funny sayings.

Rule No. 558
The popcorn purchased before the movie on the first date is always an extra large with butter.

Rule No. 559
Leave the flavored lip balms to the preteens and prostitutes.

Rule No. 560
There should definitely be a five-day waiting period for WMD's.

Rule No. 561
People who say they don't watch TV mean that they fall asleep with the TV on.

Rule No. 562
Beware the new mommy.

Rule No. 563
The fatter the friend, the more he or she will lecture you on dietary advice.

Rule No. 564
When trying on new shoes, if they pinch your feet, try this: walk out of the store in your old ones. Keep walking.

Rule No. 565
It's better to get wet than to be seen in a plastic poncho.

Rule No. 566
The shortest line will always have the slowest people.

Rule No. 567
The more sensitive the singer-songwriter, the balder the crowd.

Rule No. 568
Taking a yellow Hi-Liter to a *TV Guide* does not an academic make.

Rule No. 569
During the time one is standing above the midget urinal, one is precisely two-thirds of a man.

Rule No. 570
Anybody who says they "work hard and play hard" probably does neither.

Rule No. 571
No one ever buys the medium-sized condoms.

Rule No. 572
Horizontal stripes on your boxers will not make your penis appear larger.

Rule No. 573
No matter how poor you are, putting your pennies in rolls is, economically speaking, a waste of time.

Rule No. 574
As a group, brunette porn stars are more classically attractive than blond porn stars.

Rule No. 575
The allure of strip clubs drops dramatically when your girlfriend works in one.

Rule No. 576
Always buy your shoes after 2:00 P.M., when your feet have swollen to their maximum size.

Rule No. 577
When you die,
they will find
your porn.

Rule No. 578
Every sitcom must feature an episode in which the male character is tragically torn between celebrating a romantic milestone and using unexpected courtside basketball tickets.

Rule No. 579
The secret sauce has no turmeric.

Rule No. 580
The quality of a take-out restaurant is exactly mirrored in the quality of its napkins.

Rule No. 581
Soccer would be a lot more fun if everybody used their hands.

Rule No. 582
Denial is good, right up there with bribery.

Rule No. 583
No better cold exists than the cold of a can of beer that has been cooled by the rushing waters of a numbing stream.

Rule No. 584
One out of every four spiritual healers used to be a dental assistant.

Rule No. 585
"Lemme" is the best of the faux contractions, followed closely by "gimme."

Rule No. 586
People who laugh at their own jokes are one-tenth as funny as really unfunny people.

Rule No. 587

If you're in the delivery room and your wife's doctor says, "Take a look at this," do not, under any circumstances, take a look.

Rule No. 588

Your bumper sticker is only 3 percent as clever as you think it is.

Rule No. 589

Despite its name, the Manwich is really quite juvenile.

Rule No. 590
The adjective scrumptious should be used only by the cast of *Chitty Chitty Bang Bang*.

Rule No. 591
Beware of restaurants that have walls adorned with anchors.

Rule No. 592
There is no more extreme tyrant than the assistant manager at your local T.G.I. Friday's.

Rule No. 593
The adjective yummy should never be used to describe anything beyond food, and then only perhaps once in your adult lifetime.

Rule No. 594
Do not antagonize a man with an eye patch.

Rule No. 595
The only entity powerful enough to make a man resist pork is God.

Rule No. 596
A man should never own more than two pairs of convertible pants.

Rule No. 597
The stupider the man, the slower he walks.

Rule No. 598
When a man turns 23, it's very important he stop using the word "party" as a verb.

Rule No. 599
If you're attending a comedy show, no good can come from sitting in the front row.

Rule No. 600
The funniest tent is the yurt, followed by the tepee and the wigwam.

Rule No. 601
A man who pronounces croissants as "kwa-sa" is not a man at all.

Rule No. 602
Restaurants that demand that you call them to confirm are 73 percent more likely to have haughty servers.

Rule No. 603
Aspire to be the kind of person you've convinced your grandparents you already are.

Rule No. 604
Mail that comes in envelopes with windows is never good.

Rule No. 605
Never trust a woman who refers to her breasts as separate entities (e.g., "the girls").

Rule No. 606
Popular boys have bad posture, popular girls have good posture.

Rule No. 607
Money may not buy happiness, but it's a hefty down payment.

Rule No. 608
Toothpicks are not a viable grooming option 50 yards beyond a restaurant.

Rule No. 609
Flavored dental floss should never be sweeter than the foods that you wish to remove.

Rule No. 610
Men will travel for sex.

Rule No. 611
Men will travel for the slimmest, 1 in 1000 Hail Mary possibility of sex.

Rule No. 612
Investing in faraway banana republics with worthless currencies, dubious infrastructures, and heavily armed police is risky.

Rule No. 613
Your wife is pregnant, not "preggers" or "pregs."

Rule No. 614
No bioweapons jokes in the cover letter.

Rule No. 615
Oddly, both of the following statements are true: Monkeys are never funnier than when they're wearing clothing. And monkeys are never sadder than when they're wearing clothing.

Rule No. 616
There's no reason to feel guilty: firemen are annoying again.

Rule No. 617
A restaurant that charges a surcharge for blue cheese dressing is a restaurant to stay far away from.

Rule No. 618
When a joke is immediately followed by the phrase "Get it?", the joke's potential comedic value drops by an estimated 80 percent.

Rule No. 619
Every man should buy a round for an entire bar at least once in his life.

Rule No. 620
A man over the age of 30 should never do impressions of Austin Powers characters, most especially Fat Bastard.

Rule No. 621
There are few things sadder than a man over 40 playing air guitar.

Rule No. 622
If a young boy asks you to tell him a story, simply include a house with secret passageways and his satisfaction will be immediate.

Rule No. 623
Never trust a man wearing a Lakers jersey, a Clippers hat, and a Raiders jacket all at once.

Rule No. 624
If you ask about her previous boyfriend and she gets a small, wistful smile on her face, change the subject.

Rule No. 625
Never let a motion picture from a trans-global media conglomerate that's been test-marketed and had several scenes re-shot to hone its appeal for key target demographics touch your soul.

Rule No. 626
Less than
1 percent of
dentists
are funny.

Rule No. 627
Effigies don't have
to be anatomically
correct as long as
they're flammable.

Rule No. 628
Diplomas are not
for framing.

Rule No. 629
Any man who'd participate in an X-rated version of the Hokey Pokey is three-sixteenths of a man.

Rule No. 630
As miserable mental illnesses go, manic-depressive just sounds better than bi-polar.

Rule No. 631
It's okay to die never knowing how electric eels mate without stunning one another.

Rule No. 632
In descending order: a tad, a soupçon, a smidge.

Rule No. 633
Pigeon-toed people
are quicker than
splay-footed people.

Rule No. 634
Never order a
sloppy Joe on a
first date.

Rule No. 635
On forms where it says "sex," and you write
"yes!" they have the right to crumple up
your document and fire rubber bullets
at your groin.

Rule No. 636
All bottled water comes from a faucet in Richmond.

Rule No. 637
A man over the age of 30 should not refer to breasts as "chesticles."

Rule No. 638
You really need closer to two apples a day now to keep the doctor away.

Rule No. 639
Your fear of your boss is directly proportional to the number of boxes of Girl Scout cookies you buy from his daughter.

Rule No. 640
Lesbians make the best breakfasts.

Rule No. 641
Self-cleaning ovens usually aren't.

Rule No. 642
Scrub-free cleansing products never are.

Rule No. 643
Wrinkle-resistant trousers, oddly, actually do resist wrinkles. Unfortunately, they also resist the opposite sex.

Rule No. 644
Every man needs a pizza joint that he will vigorously defend as "The best in the world."

Rule No. 645
Pompous people like to be called pompous.

Rule No. 646
Laugh at your enemies. It couldn't possibly make things worse.

Rule No. 647
When describing the food served at a restaurant, the waiter should not use the phrase "I have a."

Rule No. 648
Words that end in "iti", "ita", or "ata" (e.g., ziti, margarita, frittata) are just plain delicious.

Rule No. 649
Barley is the most underrated grain.

Rule No. 650
Not nearly enough guys are named Rem.

Rule No. 651
Never compare someone's girlfriend or wife with an unattractive celebrity even favorably.

Rule No. 652
Never take medicine that comes in a can.

Rule No. 653
Old people always have exact change.

Rule No. 654
Expressing your creative spirit shouldn't include holding up funny signs outside morning TV shows.

Rule No. 655
Though jazz and brunch are acceptable when separated, the two should never be combined.

Rule No. 656
When it comes to air freshener, a little goes a long way.

Rule No. 657

For barbecue sauce to be your barbecue sauce, you are required to combine at least six ingredients. If the first one is Kraft Spicy Honey Barbecue Sauce, that number jumps to ten.

Rule No. 658

Unless you're in the real estate game, putting your photo on your business card is probably a bad idea.

Rule No. 659

There is no masculine way to carry a squash racket.

Rule No. 660
The dumber the man, the louder he talks.

Rule No. 661
If you purchase a paper shredder, there's an 85 percent chance that the first thing you shred will be the instructions.

Rule No. 662
You are twice as likely to get lost using GPS as you are with a paper map.

Rule No. 663
Every suburbanite under the age of 12 plays soccer; every suburbanite over the age of 16 ignores it.

Rule No. 664
If speaking to an artist or writer concerning his or her work, be as vague as possible.

Rule No. 665
Use the term blogosphere as little as possible.

Rule No. 666
It is never a good idea to compare the trajectory of your life with those of the characters in Billy Joel's "Scenes from an Italian Restaurant."

Rule No. 667
Only musicians have chops.

Rule No. 668
Relax. Enjoy
yourself. Have a
good time.

That's it!

Index

Photo Credits